Hibernal Thoughts

Kendra Townsend

Presentation by *BookLeaf Publishing*

Web: www.bookleafpub.com

E-mail: info@bookleafpub.com

ISBN: 9789357214445

First edition 2023

For Ryan,

"Scarcely had I passed them when I found him whom my soul loves. I held him, and would not let him go." Song of Solomon 3:4a

ACKNOWLEDGEMENT

My special thanks to BookLeaf Publishing for providing such an excellent writing challenge and publishing opportunity.

To my parents and brother, I am grateful for your love, friendship and endurance throughout my childhood.

To my family and friends, thank you for being present and supporting me in all my creative endeavors and for keeping me humble as needed.

To my new in-law family and friends, thank you for being there for my husband and opening your doors to this latecomer. To my Father-in-law, I could not have survived the move without your thousand small kindnesses.

To my husband, I am so thankful that you support and celebrate my talents. You are a blessing I did not expect.

To my God and Savior, thank you for healing me, leading me, and holding me fast.

PREFACE

My grandparents on both sides valued education, lifelong development. My Father's family had my grandfather, a self-taught accountant but only for his own books. He valued making things add up to his own satisfaction. My paternal Grandmother went back to college after raising her family, and became a teacher. My Mother's family had my Grandpa who only reached a high-school diploma, but read and studied, eventually becoming a pulpit supply preacher. My Maternal Grandma had only an eighth grade education, but devoted her life to learning all she could. She and my Grandpa left behind several well worn books, including poetry. While they are not here to see their granddaughter's book, I hope they would have enjoyed knowing their love of learning continues though the generations.

Midwestern Mist

The mists are cool, they envelop.
Kinder than a lover's touch.
To the eye they press in.
To the mind they are freedom.
Alone here, in the cornfield,
where stalks are all that remain,
I need not ask or answer questions.
I need apologize to no one.
I need explain nothing.
I half hope a grackle will join me,
and share its broken song,
and we can share news.
Both broken, something off,
alike but separate in our kin-doms.

The Dog passes me, fur damp,
though the mist, head to ground,
looking by nose.

The peace, the stillness,
the blankness, soothe me
and I am more myself.
The rage and and inexplicable
parts of me no one hears are freed,
and in the freeing,
tamed.

If ever another join me,
I fear they may be lost.
I fear they may be harmed.
I and the mist, though gentle,
can rend and misguide,
we are not without our dangers.
Sisters, us two.

To be lost in me is not a gift.
Why should anyone choose it?
I free the world of this obligation.
The mist is listening.
She knows I'm here, knows I have a story.
I tell her names, and she keeps them.
I tell her wishes and thoughts.
I ask her to stay, and she tries.
All is here, and nothing,
and I find the mist is home.

On Fine Nights I Walk

On fine nights I walk,
when the air agrees and
maid moon gives light,
and nobody waits for me.
I walk until the end.

The end of what?
Just..the end.
I know when and where it is,
and never bother asking why it is.

I look up, my brothers and sisters
are all there; or will be.
I will surely follow.
Thoughts come, soft and wispy,
I let them rest in my open hand.
They go when they like.

On fine nights my heart doesn't beat.
But the world is my own,
and I go home the stronger
for spending a few un-living moments
where the air, the end
and maiden moon agree.

Handwriting

Drag, friction, lines, shapes.
Something from nothing, black/white.
Pull, push, give, take...pray.

I Met You In December

I met you in December,
Though we had spoken lots,
I said hello, shared a hug.
In two days I knew,
All my hugs belonged to you.

I saw you then at Valentine's,
We sat watching the fire,
We spoke of belief and hope,
In five days I knew,
Belief and hope I shared with you.

I saw you in March,
Out on the rocks, hot coffee,
We said yes to forever.
In a single word I knew,
My earthly forever belongs with you.

Passing Thoughts

A face of marble is friendly,
But the neighbor's is not.
The graveyard holds peace,
But seldom does the sidewalks.
It is odd somehow.

The biggest dog is the kindest,
And the smallest man is cruel.
But I don't know how to help,
So I seldom ever speak.
It is sad somehow.

The softest hands and kindest words
Come from a life of scares.
I store away these gemstones
So that I can soften blows.
It is right somehow.

Life Does

Dreams never frighten me;
Life often does.
All imaginings clear my eyes;
Life often does.
Truth brings pain of infection removed;
Life often does.
Work brings about a fine soul;
Life often does.
Pain brings out the best and the worst;
Life often does.
Hope brings up the flaws;
Life always does.

What It Is

Mercy is a father's hug, a shawl on shoulders
A freeing touch of rain on upturned faces.

Pain is an endless, limping dance to hope
Casts, braces, tubes, broken attempts

Hunger is reaching for the highest branches
An iron corset that grows ever tighter

God is a crafter, slowly smoothing out the lumps
Healing the broken, reaching, hope. Granting
mercy.

Where It's Found

To find peace, look to the Northernmost Star:
Follow it to the sleeping babies and smile

To find war and murder look within you:
Tossing glass, shouting knives, a house of cards

To find history look to the used calendar:
Letters from Japan, the worn out rugs and photos

To find an Angel, look around at children's
smiles:
The friend there beside you, and the faces at
home.

Song

Paintings on the air,
Can you hear it? Can you see?
Music on the wall.

Emotion of Nothing

There is an emotion, an emotion I say,
Of nothing. A void, a blank, a vacuum, nothing.
Silver, storm-blue, brash-white, wand'ring
terracotta
Winter snow settled on Spain; both cold and
warm.
It comes with a laugh. But never mine. This;
nothing mine.
Appears, goes into my stomach; nothing from
them.
It feels good. Untouchable, unreachable, free.
Like an eagle above, but sadly alone. Empty,
A bolt of cold coffee across my tongue; not
right.
A distant touch of food—come back from
yesterday.
My nose burns like smoke and after-rain-smell
combined.
Peanut butter on a spoon. A simple scent,
There is the emotion of nothing: It is mine.
Floating in a pool, supported in my thoughts.

Childhood

Parables and whispers,
Sunlight on the grass,
Foggy days of Autumn,
Hear a figment pass.
Light and shadow shifting,
Night and day beguiled,
Not an ear can hear them,
Unless it's from a child.
Murky water faces,
Give them all a name,
So when trouble comes
We'll have someone to blame.
Blocks of leaves together
Build up fairy homes.
Toadstools all around us
Belong to all the gnomes.
Pennies made of silver,
Moons all made of gold,
Velvet hand of nighttide
Leave memories to hold.
Time will hold no meaning
While we linger here,
So let us remember clearly
And lend the past an ear.

Consolations of a Wasted Day

The walls are looking out for me:
they stopped visiting at noon,
but they will begin again at midnight.
Books and films collide in the cabinet,
running away with my fancy.
Stories, telling me how to hear them.
How to combine their seedling lessons,
to nurture as I see fit.
I have found
a magic world of shapes and lines;
sparrows that are peacocks,
like gold turned to quartz.
I can taste fresh bread and butter,
and I love the cozy solitude.

Winter

Long, white, daggers reaching from limbs.
Ice packed tight, a coyote howls.
Early for the howling.
Cold, a fast bite into cheeks.
A grip on fingers and toes;
releasing to wait for another bite
if I'm not careful.
We're old friends, Winter and I,
but he's forgetting me.
Bound to happen, I suppose,
but I miss my friend.
I breathe fast and cough the cold out.
Try again.
The magic is still there, the earth and air
that once let me see clearly.
Maybe, if I ask enough,
 they can again.

Wander

I think that life is like my auto seat,
Always, always facing front, never back.
Retracing steps, yes, but you; you can't meet.
Turn around, but never find what you lack.
Wanderlust, wanderlust, wanderlust wild,
Aren't we all looking? Oh, what a life!
Leading on, leading on, leading a child,
Aren't we all hunting, just to end strife?
Though we are seekers, we stop ourselves,
Back, looking back, to where we cannot go.
Wishing for change but back we ever delve.
And so time runs away with what we know.
We live, we learn, we try and go again,
I am glad that I shared it with you, friend.

Reaching

There is a scar on my left palm,
touching the 'life line'.
Is there a soul in the world
as displaced as me?
Seeking, hunting, unfited,
trying to find someone,
someone as I am?

Or are they in the past,
forgotten, locked in a photo
but nameless, history's dust?
Reaching, this vacancy,
always reaching.
Odd, how complete I can be
and how unwanted the world is
when I'm alone.

At the same time,
I know in the dark
I'm throwing out my hand,
tying to touch another.
Who is the scar for?
I never cut my hand,
where did it come from?

Reaching, a part of me,
bigger than anyone
I've ever met, deeper
than the local sinkhole.
This empty part that
makes me whole,
that locks me back
and sets me free.

Odd, how happy I am
when the voices on the wind
tell me of a soul they met,
and missed, when I was gone.
Strange how alone the people feel.
They are not my people.

There is a voice I search for,
an answer to a question I can't form.
It's out there, but where? But when?
That is the trouble.

I have a scar on my hand,
touching my 'life line'
with a graceful kiss,
like a loving goodbye...
reaching...
from another life.

One More

One more day,
I tell myself.
One more try,
I mutter now.
One more sigh,
I say at clock-out.
One more wish
I have in store.
One more reason,
one more season,
one more dollar,
one more holler,
one more dream,
one more scream,
one more night,
one more fight.

And someday,
one days
will be over.

So I say, just
one more time,
fighting for it to be
today, the someday,
one day that I dream.

One more day,
I tell myself,
One more door,
I haven't tried.
One more step,
I sob in silence,
One more step,
Just one more time.

And by 'one mores'
I build my life.

Christmas Mirror

Christmas is a Mirror,
we see too clearly now
what we love and fear,
but we look away somehow.

People remind us we're alone,
laughter says we're all sadder.
Sweethearts declare us on our own
the clothes say we are wider.

Songs remind us how much we care,
Bells say we've ignored a need.
The bills declare we're short on fare,
The tableware says there's mouths to feed.

But sounds remind us we are needed,
people waving says they care.
Time that passes is never quite depleted
If just a moment is taken to enjoy the air.

Christmastide is a mirror,
Double-sided, clear and true,
Careful how you look within it,
or you may find...

you have missed a life,
a life of reason,
a life of season,
a life of truth.

 Christmastide is a mirror,
Double-sided, clear and true,
Careful how you look within it,
and you may find...

You have gained a life,
a life of joy and richness.
The choice is yours,
you soon will find.

My Brother and I

Always I walk, just at this time,
The sweetest part of the day.
A little hand, once tightly in mine,
Now big and brown leads the way.

We follow the trails that we know so well,
The paths underfoot and in mind.
And as we remember and softly we tell,
A kinder future we find.

Just us, only us two,
Myself, my Brother and I.

Always our tempers fade like the day;
Always the smiles will shine.
Somehow the answer will come the same way,
If only in jokes at our time.

We're unlike the others around us it seems,
And silently hear the still hearts.
How odd and how fitting the sound in my
dreams,
The sound of our voices can't part.

Just us, only us two.
Myself, my Brother and I.

Whatever you choose, you carry my love,
My younger, my better, my friend.
Wherever you go follow the Good Guide above,
Even when roads never end.

And if at that ending you find no clear home,
And find no one wants you around,
Come back and I'll open these arms to my own,
This home need not be re-found.

Always, forever, simply,
My Brother and I.

Terrible Magnificence

When stories that were told to us
In time when we were young,
Are not to shame our innocence,
But to reflect what stung.
When looking into history
And what will still remain,
This Terrible Magnificence
Is freedom born of pain.

When darkest dreaming writhe, awake,
And inner voices shrieking louder still,
Chained up and fed, but slimmly so,
And fierce grows our heart's refill.
When kindness keeps our beast at bay,
But not out of our thoughts,
This Terrible Magnificence
Is power left unsought.

We give our warning clear, but soft,
And live out moral lives,
We feel lost, but stand sure and firmly,
So others aren't lost in daily strife.
They'll needle, wheedle, poke and say,
"We push, but don't you rage or rife!"
This Terrible Magnificence
Will rush out truth for all our lives.

A terrifying thing to know and see yourself,
To take distant peace that costs so dear,
To know your darkest and your lightest,
And know the path so freely clear
They'll wonder are you right or wrong,
And put the blame on all you are and do,
My Terrible Magnificence
Could bless or curse, that's up to you.

Winter Kisses

Coldest kisses from the snow
Showered to the Earth below.
So different from the summer rain,
that over-loves in lavish gain.

Winter wonders catch the eye,
Snow snakes walking, birds fly high,
the hoarfrost coats the plants around,
and fox tracks show the safest ground.

To travel in this gentle world,
To watch a healing show unfurled
It's a joy that few can know,
If hurry is the way they go.

So take a step, and walk with me,
no fear in chilly harmony
hear secret songs from bird and beast,
winter wishes, snow kissed, hope released

Beloved

The Unexpected
The Reliable
The beautiful
The Wild
The ever changing patterns of life

A sound
A Laugh
A Door
A Light
The ever familiar framework of a day

Your kindness
Your faith
Your hope
Your honesty
The ever growing inner world

My will
My thoughts
My dreams
My understanding
The ever developing soul

Your warmth
Your strength
Your smile
Your presence
The ever joyful reliability

Our path
Our tears
Our life
Our purpose
This all and more is why
you are my Beloved